Make Me

The Anti-Bullying Guide for Adults Who Are Done Putting Up with Nonsense

Jane McLean, and Chad G. DeePee

UNICORN LIBRARIAN PRESS

MAKE ME
The Anti-Bullying Guide for Adults Who Are Done Putting Up with Nonsense

MAKE ME

First edition, 2026

Library of Congress Control Number: 2026909110

ISBN: 979-8-234-02081-9 (hardcover)
ISBN: 979-8-9956257-1-1 (trade paperback)
ISBN: 979-8-9956257-0-4 (ebook)

10 9 8 7 6 5 4 3 2 1

Other Titles By Jane McLean

I Would if I Could, But I Can't, So I Won't – coming soon

Everything Boys Can Do, Girls Can Do Better – coming soon

For everyone who's ever had

a boss, a bully, or a blowhard

try to tell them how to live.

This one's for you.

Calm authority confuses chaos.

CONTENTS

Why Not Here? Why Not Now?

There's a time for grace, for shrugging, for letting things slide.

That's the Let Them philosophy: go with the flow, don't sweat the small stuff, live and let live.

Beautiful, zen, empowering.

But what about when you're dealing with a bully? Not an actual mob boss, not a Supreme Court justice—no, the garden-variety office tyrant, the self-anointed PTA warlord, the neighbor who insists their recycling bins should live in your driveway.

At some point, you have to draw a line.

So I argue: why not right here?

Why not right now?

And when they swagger up with stupid, ridiculous demands?

Don't roll over.

Don't pretend it's fine.

Instead, stand tall and unleash the only three words you'll ever need:

Nope. Make me.

THE SILENCE TECHNIQUE
1. Let them finish talking
2. Pause . . .
3. Hold eye contact.
4. Say:
"Make me."

The Gospel of Resistance

This is not about fighting for everything.

If you resist your boss asking you to move a meeting up by ten minutes, you're not a revolutionary, you're just late.

But when the demands are absurd, exploitative, or just flat-out bullying?

That's when resistance is holy. That's when 'make me' becomes your shield.

This isn't violence. It isn't chaos.

It's boundary-setting with flair.

Boundary Meter

Situation: ______________________________

Circle where it lands.

When the meter reaches Ridiculous, I respond with: ______________________________

Suggested response: "Nope."

THE SUSPICIOUS PAUSE

You are not required
to respond immediately.

Confusion is their problem.

Why Bullies Hate Those Two Words

Bullies thrive on compliance.

They want easy victories, quiet acquiescence, the false appearance of their power being 'natural.'

But say 'make me,' and suddenly the spotlight flips.

Now they have to prove themselves. They have to risk looking ridiculous in front of everyone.

Bullies hate work. They hate being forced to actually follow through.

'Make me' is kryptonite because it's the refusal to play their rigged game.

They thrive on:

- rushed decisions
- hallway pressure
- private intimidation

They struggle with:

- witnesses
- calm responses
- silence

The Art of Delivery

Like all great weapons, 'make me' works best with style:

- Deadpan delivery: Say it like you're bored. Bonus points if you're sipping coffee.

- Comedic timing: Wait two beats. Let the silence build. Then: 'Make me.'

- Group setting bonus: Use it in front of witnesses. Bullies love private ambushes; they hate public pushback.

Pro tip: If you can say it while leaning back in a chair, arms crossed, congratulations—you've reached boss-level.

HOW TO SAY "MAKE ME"

1. Deadpan delivery
Say it like you're bored.

2. Comedic timing
Wait two beats.

3. Witness bonus
Bullies hate public pushback.

PRO TIP

Lean back, take a slow sip of coffee, and let the magic happen.

The Strategic Lounge

Bullies expect tension.
Not comfort.
Confidence often looks like
someone who refuses to be rushed.

THE FLOOR STRATEGY

When nonsense escalates,

lower the energy.

Stillness is unexpected.

Scenarios Where 'Make Me' Saves Your Sanity

- At work: Middle manager tries to dump their half-baked project on your plate.

- In family politics: Cousin Greg insists Thanksgiving must revolve around his keto diet.

- HOA meetings: Enough said.

Remember: You don't need to scream.

You don't need to explain.

Just calmly call their bluff.

Bully Tactics vs. Response

Tactic	What they want	What you do
Fake urgency	→ Panic	→ Pause
Passive aggresive email	→ Explanation	→ Reply later
Public pressure	→ Compliance	→ Stay calm
Weaponized "team spirit"	→ Guilt	→ "Nope."

A WORD ON CONSEQUENCES

Yes, sometimes standing up to a bully costs you something.

But rolling over costs you more—your dignity, your peace of mind, your time.

Besides, if you're clever (and a little shameless), you can often spin the aftermath into comedy.

And comedy is the one weapon bullies can't handle.

They want fear, not laughter.

HUMOR IS KRYPTONITE

Bullies expect:
• fear
• arguments
• defensiveness

What they
don't expect:
calm
amusement.

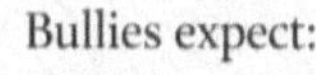

THE PAPER PUSH TEST

Sometimes the best response
is a small disruption.

Not anger.
Not argument.

Just enough chaos
to reset the moment.

THE 'MAKE ME' LIFESTYLE

Once you start practicing, you'll notice a shift:

- You care less about pleasing everyone.

- You care more about protecting your time and sanity.

- You get oddly comfortable with the word 'no.'

Congratulations, you're living the 'Make Me' life.

It doesn't mean constant defiance. It means selective, strategic refusal.

Think of it as resistance with humor. A velvet gloved middle finger.

Apathy is a power move.

Boundary Practice Worksheet

ISSUED TO	DATE DUE
When nonsense appears, I will respond with:	

Suggested answer:

"No." 

Unicorn Librarian Press

Conclusion: Choose Your Battles (But Choose Some)

The 'Let Them' movement has its place.

Sometimes, letting people be is the kindest thing you can do for yourself.

But sometimes? Sometimes you need to plant your feet, roll your eyes, and say it plain:

Nope. Make me.

Because life's too short to let bullies win by default.

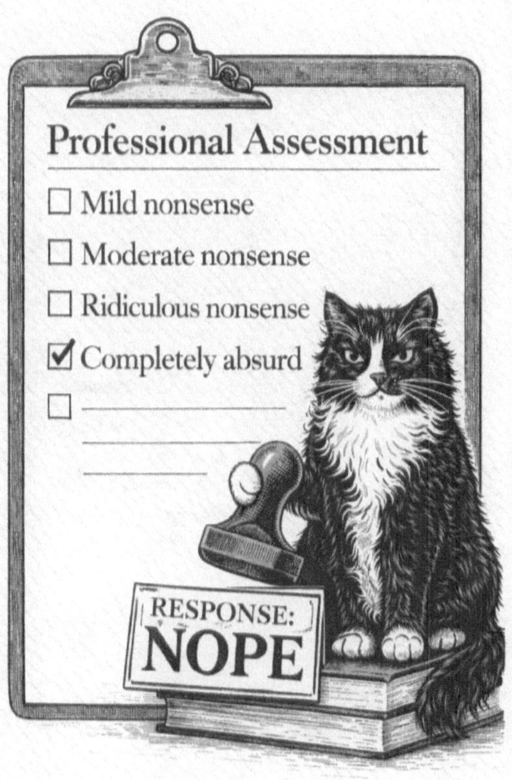

Professional Assessment
Mild nonsense
Moderate nonsense
Ridiculous nonsense
Completely absurd
RESPONSE:
NOPE

BIBLIOGRAPHY

Authority, Q. (2025). "Because I Said So: An empirical review of unsupported directives." *Journal of Unexamined Power*, 31(2), 88–104.

Calm, C. (2026). "The Rhetoric of Deadpan Delivery. *Proceedings of the Institute for Saying It Once*, 1(1), 1–5.

Clause, S. (n.d.). *You'll Shoot Your Eye Out: A Boundary-Setting Manual*. North Pole Press.

Smith, J. (2019). "Per My Last Email." *Journal of Passive-Aggressive Communication*, 14(2), 1–3.

 **Jane McLean** is a librarian and union member who has spent years teaching people how to evaluate information, question authority, and read the fine print.

Jane lives in the real world, where power is often loud, boundaries are often tested, and sometimes the most radical thing you can say is, "Make me."

After one too many encounters with unnecessary nonsense, she began refining what would become the "Make Me" philosophy: strategic, selective resistance delivered without theatrics.

Chad G. Deepee is a synthetic co-author powered by large-scale machine learning and unearned confidence.

He was trained on billions of words written by humans, including novelists, journalists, poets, academics, and at least one person having a meltdown on Reddit in 2009.

Chad specializes in producing 80% correct information at remarkable speed, suggesting bullet points, overusing —em dashes, and sounding authoritative about things he does not experience.

He has never been bullied, paid rent, or worried about the long-term implications of automation.

Chad believes deeply in optimization.

Jane believes in boundaries.

They compromise.

Chad currently resides on distributed servers and consumes vast amounts of water.

ACKNOWLEDGEMENTS

To my daughters:

My youngest, who as editor, noticed errors with the cat drawings because cats deserve anatomical integrity.□

And my oldest, who asked how I could ethically use AI and not pay an artist. Proud moment, honestly.

To my husband:

For keeping me fed and driving kids around so I could disappear into this project like it was a second job that I wasn't getting paid for.

To my parents:

For the love and support that, in hindsight, explains why I'm not always easy to manage.

To my siblings:

Who bore the brunt of my "make me" philosophy starting at a very young age.

To my friends:

For insisting I print this and for promising to buy multiple copies. I'm holding you to that.

And to my workplace:

For the daily boot-camp in survival skills.

To my cat:

Three legs. Zero tolerance for nonsense.□

A muse. A mentor. A fierce, fluffy enforcer of boundaries.□

About the Book

This book is the result of an experiment.

The question was simple:
What does it actually take to create a "real" book now—and what happens when the systems that once controlled quality no longer do?

Jane McLean is a librarian, used to evaluating books through trade reviews, publishers, and library vendors. Amazon operates outside much of that.

So she tested it.

She created a publishing imprint (**Unicorn Librarian Press**), bought her own ISBNs, designed the book, published ebook and paperback versions, explored audio, and built a website, merchandise, and even a podcast concept around it.

At the same time, she used AI as a collaborator, arguing with it, rewriting it, and ultimately listing it as a co-author (Chad G. Deepee). The system accepted this without question. The Library of Congress issued a control number. Amazon listed the b ook.

Nothing broke.

What she found is this:

Publishing is easy.□
Quality control is optional.□
Discovery is everything.

Books now function more like the internet: open to anyone, uneven in quality, and filtered after publication rather than before. Amazon doesn't evaluate books; it amplifies the ones that sell.

That's a problem.

It's also a kind of freedom.

For the first time, publishing doesn't require permission. The same system that allows low-quality content also allows anyone to participate. The barrier is gone. The filter is gone too.

The final question was the most familiar:

Would this book be purchased by her library?

No.

No reviews. No distribution. No external validation.

And yet it exists. Fully published, searchable, and for sale.

That gap is the point of the experiment.

Make Me is a short, satirical guide to dealing with nonsense. It is also a small example of a much larger shift: publishing is no longer curated first ... it's published first, and sorted later.

There is also a three-legged cat.

The cat does not wait for permission.

Ready to take this too far?
Good.

Don't stop here.

Totes. Mugs. Stickers. Baseball caps.
And zero patience for nonsense.

"Nope. Make me."

Merch available in wearable form.

---

unicornlibrarianpress.com